D0118787

James Watt
and the Steam Engine

Mitchell Lane
PUBLISHERS

P.O. Box 196
Hockessin, Delaware
19707

Titles in the Series

Visit us on the web: www.mitchelllane.com
Comments? email us: mitchelllane@mitchelllane.com

Uncharted, Unexplored, and Unexplained

Scientific Advancements of the 19th Century

James Watt
and the Steam Engine

Jim Whiting

Uncharted, Unexplored, and Unexplained

Scientific Advancements of the 19th Century

Copyright © 2006 by Mitchell Lane Publishers, Inc. All rights reserved. No part of this book may be reproduced without written permission from the publisher. Printed and bound in the United States of America.

Printing   1   2   3   4   5   6   7   8   9

Library of Congress Cataloging-in-Publication Data
Whiting, Jim, 1943–
    James Watt and the steam engine / by Jim Whiting.
        p. cm. — (Uncharted, unexplored, and unexplained)
    Includes bibliographical references and index.
    ISBN 1-58415-371-7 (library bound)
1. Watt, James, 1736–1819—Juvenile literature. 2. Mechanical Engineers—Great Britain—Biography—Juvenile literature. [1. Inventors.] I.Title. II. Series.
    TJ140.W38.W3 2005
    621'.092—dc22
                                                                    2005009694

ABOUT THE AUTHOR: Jim Whiting has been a remarkably versatile and accomplished journalist, writer, editor, and photographer for more than 30 years. A voracious reader since early childhood, Mr. Whiting has written and edited about 200 nonfiction children's books. His subjects range from authors to zoologists and include contemporary pop icons and classical musicians, saints and scientists, emperors and explorers. Representative titles include *The Life and Times of Franz Liszt*, *The Life and Times of Julius Caesar*, *Charles Schulz*, and *Juan Ponce de Leon*.

Other career highlights are a lengthy stint publishing *Northwest Runner*, the first piece of original fiction to appear in *Runners World* magazine, hundreds of descriptions and venue photographs for America Online, e-commerce product writing, sports editor for the *Bainbridge Island Review*, light verse in a number of magazines and acting as the official photographer of the Antarctica Marathon.

He lives in Washington state with his wife and two teenage sons.

PHOTO CREDITS: Cover, pp. 1, 3—Mary Evans Picture Library; p. 6—Jamie Kondrchek; p.10—Superstock; p. 14 —Corbis; p. 16—Photo Researchers; p. 18—Jamie Kondrchek; p. 22—Getty Images; p. 25—Science Museum/Science and Society Picture Library; p. 30—Photo Researchers; p. 33—Corbis; p. 35—Andrea Pickens; p. 38—Mary Evans Picture Library; p. 41—Library of Congress

PUBLISHER'S NOTE: This story is based on the author's extensive research, which he believes to be accurate. Documentation of such research is on page 46. The internet sites referenced herein were active as of the publication date. Due to the fleeting nature of some websites, we cannot guarantee they will all be active when you are reading this book.

Uncharted, Unexplored, and Unexplained

Scientific Advancements of the 19th Century

James Watt
and the Steam Engine

Before the Industrial Revolution, mills were powered by water running over waterwheels. The wheel turned a shaft at its center, which drove machinery inside the building.

1

A Momentous Change

If an Englishman from the time of Robin Hood—which was most likely sometime in the 1200s—could have boarded a time machine and vaulted ahead five centuries, he would have noticed a few changes in his country. Even though the language the people spoke would still have been called "English," he would have had trouble understanding it because so many words were different. Towns were larger. So were some of the buildings. Clothing styles would have changed as well.

But in many other respects, the earlier man would have felt at home. Most people still lived in the countryside or in small villages. They were unlikely to venture far from home because the roads were still rough, unpaved, and often muddy. The tools they used in their daily tasks were virtually unchanged from those of Robin Hood's time. While the clothing they wore may have been different, the way in which most of it was made was almost the same. People raised sheep, sheared them, spun the wool into thread, then made the thread into cloth. The relatively few factories that existed had to be built next to streams or rivers. They ran on power from waterwheels that turned from the force of the current.

Another similarity would have been the pace of life. On land, people still traveled on foot or horseback. At sea, ships were driven by the wind, as they had been for hundreds of years. Of course, if there was no wind, the ships went nowhere.

This stable way of life was about to undergo a monumental change. Within a short period of time, the way in which people lived and worked would be completely transformed. This transformation came to be called the Industrial Revolution.

A number of technological advancements made the Industrial Revolution possible. None was more important than the steam engine. Steam power was not a new phenomenon—Hero of Alexandria had constructed a primitive toy steam engine during the first century A.D.—yet no one had understood how to harness it for practical purposes until quite recently. The time traveler might have noticed a few massive steam engines (or "fire engines," as they were more commonly known), but they were inefficient and had very limited uses.

Within the space of a few decades at the end of the 18th century, steam engines would shed these limitations. Hundreds would begin to power the huge factories that seemed to spring up almost overnight, creating tens of thousands of jobs and changing England from an agricultural, rural society to one that was industrial and urban.

No one is more closely connected with this transformation of the steam engine than James Watt. While Watt did not invent the steam engine, as some people erroneously believe, he conceived and then perfected the changes that were necessary for it to fulfill its vast potential.

He was a somewhat reluctant revolutionary. Prone to fits of depression and self-doubt, he was ready to abandon his work with steam on more than one occasion. Fortunately he had devoted friends who believed in him and in what he was capable of achieving. They encouraged him to keep going.

By the end of his life he was one of the most famous men in England. As a measure of his importance, he has a memorial in Westminster Abbey, alongside England's other most noted scientific, literary, and political figures. It identifies him as "among the most illustrious followers of science and the real benefactors of the world."[1]

Revolution

Historians agree about the starting dates for some revolutions. The American Revolution, for example, began with the battles of Lexington and Concord on April 18, 1775. The French Revolution began with the storming of the Bastille prison on July 14, 1789.

There is, however, little agreement about the beginning of the Industrial Revolution in England. Some historians maintain that it began early in the 18th century, while others put its origins several decades later. But there is complete agreement about its effects. It transformed England into one of the world's most powerful nations.

John Kay

Historians also agree that the term "Industrial Revolution" is somewhat misleading, because it suggests a sudden change. In reality, the Industrial Revolution developed over a period of up to 100 years and involved changes—many of them gradual—in a number of areas.

One step on the way was Jethro Tull's invention of the seed drill in 1701. This drill allowed farmers to drastically increase the yields of their crops. The extra food helped to feed the growing population of England.

Another was the development of a method of smelting large quantities of high-quality iron. Three generations of the Abraham Darby family, beginning in 1709, worked on this technology. The iron was used for cylinders in Watt's engines, as the framework for building increasingly larger factories, in improved tools, and for building bridges, railroads, and ships.

Then came a series of inventions that completely changed the textile industry. For centuries, textile manufacturing had been a "cottage industry." Individuals produced fabrics in their homes (or cottages). Starting in 1733 with John Kay's flying shuttle (which was used for weaving), these inventions took the production and weaving of textiles out of people's homes and into large and complex factories. These factories became a major market for Watt's steam engines.

By 1800, the industrial production of textiles, from raw materials through finished product, was running smoothly. Coupled with numerous other advances, these changes paved the way for the growth and development of the British Empire. By the end of the century, it would span the entire globe.

Watt Discovering Condensation of Steam, painted by Marcus Stone (1840–1921). Many people believe that James Watt's interest in steam began when he was a young boy. He watched the lid of a teapot as it bobbed up and down. He realized that the steam produced by the boiling water was causing the lid to move.

A Perplexing Problem

For Agnes and James Watt, the birth of a son on January 19, 1736, was cause for joy. But it was a very cautious joy. In more than six years of marriage, the couple had had several children already. None had survived past infancy.

They named the little boy James after his father. James Senior was one of the leading citizens of the Scottish coastal town of Greenock. He was a merchant, carpenter, cabinetmaker, and shipbuilder. He owned a part interest in several of the vessels he had helped to launch. Agnes Watt, as was customary in that era, was a homemaker.

With the deaths of her other children still weighing heavily on her mind, Agnes must have been especially sensitive to the needs of the baby. Little James wasn't very strong. From an early age, he suffered from migraine headaches, a problem that plagued him for the rest of his life. He was often ill as he grew older. Because of his health problems, he wasn't able to go outside and play very much with other children his age. Because he was indoors so much, James read a great deal. His mother homeschooled him for a few years. It must have been a shock when he finally began attending school with other children. His stronger classmates bullied him, and he didn't do well in his studies.

Unlike many shy, bookish youngsters, however, James was very good with his hands. His father recognized this talent and made space for his son in the workshop at his shipyard. He set up a little forge and lathe for James, as well as a workbench that was well stocked with tools. The boy quickly mastered everything he had been given. He spent a lot of time with the navigational instruments that were so important to the seafarers who came to the shipyard. He was especially interested in learning about their inner workings. He also enjoyed making models of the cranes that were used to lift cargo on and off the sailing ships that dotted the harbor. He even made a small barrel organ.

His work was so good that he became a perfectionist. In later life he would get angry at others' poor workmanship.

His school situation took a turn for the better when he switched schools at age 13. He learned a little Latin and Greek, and did especially well in geometry. This wasn't entirely a surprise, because his grandfather had been a mathematics teacher.

As was common at the time, the elder James expected his son to take over the family business. But what may have seemed to be a smooth path for the teenager soon hit a couple of major roadblocks. The first came in 1753 with the death of his mother. Soon afterward, one of his father's ships was wrecked and the business suffered a downturn. In the resulting turmoil, James persuaded his father to allow him to take advantage of his skill with his hands. He wanted to become an instrument maker instead of a merchant. He would have to serve as an apprentice in order to learn the trade. In the summer of 1754, James packed a few of his possessions and headed for Glasgow, a much larger seaport in western Scotland. Some of his mother's relatives lived there and offered him a room while he pursued his craft.

He spent the next year in Glasgow, though it isn't clear how much he learned. While he was there, one of his relatives introduced him to Dr. Robert Dick, a professor of natural philosophy at Glasgow University. Dick recognized James's ability and urged him to go to London, the leading city in Europe for making instruments. He would receive much better training there.

It took James and a friend nearly two weeks to make the long trip, but the difficulties of the journey paled in comparison with what came next. No one would take him on as an apprentice. Even worse, James— still somewhat frail—lived in constant fear of the press gangs that roamed the city streets. These gangs rounded up "volunteers" for the rough life of a seaman in the Royal Navy. Finally he was introduced to John Morgan, a versatile instrument maker. Morgan agreed to work with him.

With the benefit of all the happy hours that he had spent in his father's shop, James made rapid progress. He had to. The normal course of training to become an instrument maker was four years. James had only one. He often worked from just after dawn until eight or nine in the evening. His hard work paid off. He made rapid progress. He even began to think about starting his own business.

This success came at a cost. Concern about the press gangs and long hours of work kept him cooped up inside most of the time. He didn't have much money, so he often didn't eat very well. As a result, he was racked with severe backaches and other physical ailments during his last months in London.

James returned to Greenock in 1756, hoping to regain his health and to begin working as an instrument maker. His friend Robert Dick helped him out again. A wealthy merchant named Alexander Macfarlane had returned to Glasgow from Jamaica with a number of valuable astronomical instruments. He donated them to Glasgow University to help establish an observatory. Unfortunately, several weeks at sea had exposed the instruments to damaging salt water. At Dick's recommendation, James was hired to repair them. He was also given a place to stay at the university while he worked on the instruments.

James became friends with John Anderson, a professor at the university who helped him capitalize on his work with Macfarlane's instruments. At Anderson's insistence, James was appointed Mathematical Instrument Maker to the University. The appointment also included a comfortable apartment.

Joseph Black (1728–1799) was an important influence on the young James Watt. Black received early training in medicine and remained a physician for the rest of his life. He also taught at Glasgow University (1756–1766) and then at Edinburgh. He made important discoveries about the characteristics of carbon dioxide and heat, and was a popular lecturer in the field of chemistry.

During this time, James met a noted professor of chemistry named Joseph Black and a student named John Robison. Both men became lifelong friends. Black was an important figure in 18th-century science. He did groundbreaking research into the characteristics of heat and of carbon dioxide, which he called "fixed air." Black often called on James to make and repair equipment for his lectures.

In 1759, Robison developed an interest in steam power. Like a number of other people of that era, he believed that steam could be used to propel wagons. He asked James to make a model. James confessed that he knew almost nothing about steam, but agreed to try. His model didn't work.

Watt wasn't accustomed to failure. He began reading about some of the early experiments with steam, though time for such reading was a luxury. He had to make a living. His work at the university wasn't very lucrative, so he opened an instrument-making shop in Glasgow. To help finance the shop, he formed a partnership with Glasgow architect John Craig.

His shop did well enough that he could open an even larger one in 1763. At one point, he had 16 people working for him. One of his main projects was an organ, somewhat to the amazement of his friends. They commented on his almost complete ignorance of music. "We all knew he could not tell one musical note from another," Robison said.[1] Characteristically, he immersed himself in the subject and his organ worked perfectly.

In 1764, he was successful enough that he could marry his cousin Margaret Miller, who was better known as Peggy. As historian Jenny Uglow notes, "The only person who made Watt genuinely light-hearted, Peggy eased his life; his headaches lessened, his panics and depressions calmed. In letter after letter, she told him to look after himself, to keep warm, not to worry, to come home soon, and she kept the shop while he was away, taking orders and dealing with clients."[2]

James, like his father, seemed destined to become a pillar of the community with a successful business. But a combination of his own natural curiosity and a series of outside events soon propelled his life in an entirely different direction.

As England's population grew, it needed a steadily increasing amount of coal for heating during the sometimes harsh winters. As miners dug deeper into the earth, they encountered a problem. Groundwater would seep into the mines, making it much more difficult to extract the coal.

The first solution for getting rid of the excess water was using a series of buckets. Horses provided the power to lift them. This was a slow process. It was also expensive because the horses required food and shelter.

In 1698, an engineer named Thomas Savery invented a steam pump that had some success in solving the water problem. It consisted of a boiler connected to a large tank. Steam from the boiler would be piped

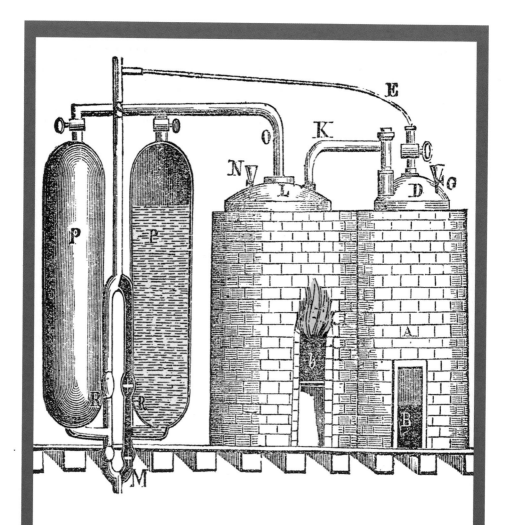

A diagram of Thomas Savery's steam pump. The boilers (at right) produced steam. They were connected to the steam vessels (P). Alternately cooling and heating the vessels pulled up water and drained it. Using two vessels allowed the pumping action to be continuous.

into the tank. Then the tank would be cooled and the steam would condense, creating a vacuum. At that point, a pipe from the tank leading into the flooded mine would open. The vacuum in the tank would draw the water upward into the tank. Fresh steam from the boiler would enter the tank, forcing the water to the surface. Savery called his invention the Miner's Friend and advertised it as "the engine for raising water by fire."

The "Miner's Friend" had serious drawbacks. It could work only in shallow mines. It couldn't draw much water. Because of the steam pressure needed to raise the water high enough, dangerous boiler explosions were common.

Fourteen years later, Thomas Newcomen invented a steam engine that worked much better than Savery's. It pumped out far more water. The heart of the engine was a large cylinder mounted on top of a boiler. Inside the cylinder was a piston, which was connected by a chain to one end of a massive wooden beam. The other, heavier end of the beam was connected to a pump.

At rest, the pump end of the beam would be down and the piston would be at the top of the cylinder. A valve under the cylinder would open and steam from the boiler would rush into the cylinder. Then that valve would close and another valve, connected to a cistern containing cold water, would open. The cold water would enter the cylinder and condense the steam, creating a vacuum at the bottom of the cylinder. Atmospheric pressure would force the piston down, which in turn would pull down the end of the beam to which it was fastened. The other end of the beam would rise, pumping water out of the ground. When the piston reached the bottom of the cylinder, gravity would force down the heavier pump end of the beam. The end connected to the piston would begin to rise again, pulling the piston upward. The valve from the boiler would open, admitting another gust of steam, and the process would begin all over.

While the theory of operation was simple, the "fire engines" themselves were complicated. They were also inefficient. The cylinder had to be kept hot while it was filling with steam, then quickly cooled to condense the steam. Before the next stroke could begin, the cylinder

A model of Thomas Newcomen's steam engine. The boiler (lower right) generated steam. The cylinder just above the boiler moved up and down. In turn, the beam to which it was connected also moved up and down. Its up stroke would pump water out of the mines.

had to be heated again. As a result, much of the steam that came in at the start of the next cycle was used to reheat the cylinder. Even more steam was necessary to fill the cylinder as the piston rose upward. This made the operation of the pump very slow. It also required a great deal of energy because of the amount of steam that had to be produced. Some Newcomen engines used up to 13 tons of coal every day.

Despite its inefficiencies, however, the Newcomen engine was relatively successful. Within two decades of its introduction, dozens were in use. Even though they burned a great deal of coal, they allowed miners to go ever deeper in their search for coal. The bottom line was that they helped to produce more coal than they consumed.

Watt was familiar with the Newcomen engine. He had read about it after he'd tried to construct a working model of a steam-driven wagon. He had also done experiments with steam. In 1763, he had the chance to do a practical test. The university owned a model of the Newcomen engine, which was used in classroom demonstrations. Unfortunately, it had stopped working. The governing board of the university assigned Anderson the task of making it work again. Anderson didn't have any difficulty deciding on the right man for the job. It was his friend James Watt.

Watt quickly found the problem with the model and made it work again. As an instrument maker who was used to doing quality work, it upset him that the model was not particularly well made. He was also concerned about how inefficient it was. The boiler was so small that it emptied rapidly. As a result, the model would stop after only a few strokes. He wanted to improve the little machine. He made several alterations, trying to get it to run longer. Nothing worked. There didn't seem to be any way around the basic problem: The continual cycle of heating/cooling/reheating used up so much steam that the boiler ran dry too fast.

The problem became virtually an obsession. He spent a great deal of his limited spare time working on it. Months passed with almost no improvement. Then one day in the spring of 1765, he had a flash of inspiration. It made such a strong impression on him that he could vividly recall the details nearly four decades later. Today, a boulder with an inscription marks the exact place where inspiration struck.

"I had gone to take a walk on a fine Sabbath afternoon," he told a young engineer who greatly admired his work. "I had entered the Green by the gate at the foot of Charlotte Street—had passed the old washing-house. I was thinking upon the engine at the time and had gone as far as the Herd's house when the idea came into my mind, that as steam was an elastic body it would rush into a vacuum, and if a communication was made between the cylinder and an exhausted vessel, it would rush into it, and might be there condensed without cooling the cylinder. . . . I had not walked further than the Gold-house when the whole thing was arranged in my mind."[3]

In other words, he would allow the steam to flow into a separate condenser, where it could be cooled. That would create a vacuum inside the main cylinder while still allowing the cylinder to retain the necessary heat.

The next day he went to work on his idea. Within a few days he had constructed a working model. The steam came out of the cylinder and flowed into a separate condenser, just as he had envisioned. A layer of insulation kept the cylinder itself hot. Now the "fire engine" could keep going much longer.

It was a start. It wasn't even close to the finish.

for the Royal Navy

James Watt's worries about being forced into serving in the Royal Navy were well founded. When he arrived in London, France and England had just gone to war. There weren't enough volunteers to fill the crews of Royal Navy warships. This wasn't surprising.

Even in peacetime, life at sea was uncomfortable. The men were packed tightly together; they worked very hard for very little pay; the food was terrible; they endured harsh discipline, getting flogged for even minor offenses; and there was the ever-present danger of falling while working high aloft on the towering masts.

Sailors, including these men from World War II, have traditionally slept in cramped quarters.

Wartime only increased the dangers. Cannonballs could rip men's heads off, jagged wooden splinters several feet long could impale them, and sharpshooters on enemy ships could pick off crew members.

The Royal Navy was responsible for keeping open the sea lanes to England, an island nation. The Impress Service was established to make sure that there were enough sailors to man its ships at all times. Based on the king's legal right to draft men for military service, the service set up a headquarters (called a rendezvous) in every major port. Each was under the command of a regulating officer. The officer would hire some of the local thugs to form press gangs. These men had an additional incentive for joining. As press gang members, they didn't run the risk of being impressed themselves. While they didn't receive much money for their work, some of their frightened victims offered them significant amounts of money to leave them alone.

Press gangs found many of their "recruits" in taverns. Often they would get them so drunk that they passed out. When the victims awoke, they would already be at sea. At other times the gangs had to employ more aggressive measures, pulling men off the streets and literally kidnapping them.

When the wars with French emperor Napoléon ended in 1815, British impressment steadily declined. But the laws authorizing it have never been repealed.

James Watt studies a model of Thomas Newcomen's steam engine. Fixing it was easy. Improving it would change the course of history.

3

Trials and Tribulations

It was one thing to build a model. It was something entirely different to build a full-size machine that would work in the real world. Watt knew that to develop the machine, he would need a great deal of money—far more money than what his shop could bring in.

One possibility was his business partner Craig, but in December 1765, Craig died. Watt not only lost his financial backing, but he also had to sell part of his business in order to pay Craig's heirs.

Black was another possibility. While he offered what he could, he was not particularly rich. Then Black had an idea. He could ask his wealthy friend John Roebuck, who had supported other projects that had generated impressive returns. There was another reason for Roebuck to be interested. Roebuck had just embarked on an ambitious coal mining venture at Kinneil, about 20 miles northeast of Glasgow. His new mines were taking on a great deal of water. He didn't believe that a Newcomen engine could keep up with the inflow. Watt's new engine could offer the solution. It seemed to be an ideal match of inventor and consumer.

There was another reason to hope for success. Watt was easily discouraged when he ran into problems. Roebuck was the opposite. He had a lot of energy and was willing to push ahead even when things didn't work right away.

Unfortunately, Roebuck was facing financial difficulties. He couldn't offer much more than his energy. When Watt began assembling an engine at the site of Roebuck's mine, a dizzying series of technical problems quickly arose. After a number of failures, Watt became discouraged.

At that time, English roads were of relatively poor quality. In wet weather, they often became so muddy that transportation literally bogged down. As a result, waterways were the most reliable method of moving large quantities of goods. Entrepreneurs dreamed of linking the country's rivers with a series of canals. They needed land surveyors to study possible routes.

Watt's first child, John, had died soon after being born in 1765. Watt wanted others. He knew he had to find a steady income to support a family. He decided to become a surveyor. The steam engine would have to wait.

Watt found work studying a possible canal route from the Firth of Forth, an estuary off the North Sea, to the Clyde River. He went to London to try to persuade the English Parliament to support the project. He failed; another route was chosen. However, the trip had an unexpected side benefit. Watt stopped in the city of Birmingham on the way back. He met two men, Erasmus Darwin and William Small, both of whom became his close friends. The friendship of Small—who had lived in the American colonies and profoundly influenced such eminent Americans as Thomas Jefferson and Benjamin Franklin—would become of inestimable value. He often encouraged Watt, whose fits of depression continued to handicap his ability to work.

Somehow Watt managed to find time to work on the steam engine. He made enough progress to convince Roebuck to provide some financial backing. Roebuck drove a stiff bargain. In return for paying off Watt's debts and offering additional funds, he became a two-thirds partner. He owned two-thirds of the assets and would receive two-thirds of whatever profits the engine would make. To protect themselves, the two men agreed that Watt needed to patent his condenser. A patent is a document that gives an inventor the sole right to use or sell his or her invention for a certain period of time. Late in 1768, Watt set off for London to file the necessary paperwork.

Once again he stopped at Birmingham on the way back. Since his previous visit, his friend William Small had become the personal physician to Matthew Boulton, one of the leading manufacturers of the era. Boulton had inherited a belt buckle business from his father. A man who "thought big," he had gone far beyond his original product to produce a wide-ranging assortment of "toys": watch chains, sword hilts, fancy buttons, and much

Matthew Boulton was the ideal partner for James Watt. He had financial resources, a forceful personality, and a vision of the future. Like Watt, he also had the commitment to produce first-rate work.

more. Even more notable, he produced these goods in a massive state-of-the-art manufacturing facility known as Soho. He employed more than 600 highly skilled craftsmen. One of Boulton's intentions was to prove that a "provincial" city such as Birmingham could produce first-rate work. He succeeded. Today many of the items produced there are displayed in museums.

Boulton had a problem. A portion of his factory used machinery powered by a waterwheel driven by the flow of a stream. The flow slowed in summer, when the water level was lower, and in winter, when the stream froze over. At those times, he had to bring in horses to pump water into the stream from wells.

Boulton was considering buying a Newcomen machine. Small told him about James Watt and the steam engine he was trying to build. Boulton immediately realized the possibilities that an improved engine offered. He rolled out the red carpet for his visitor. Watt was his guest for two weeks, spending enough time with Boulton to realize that Boulton shared his commitment to quality work and that Soho could easily become the home of his steam engine. As soon as he returned to Glasgow, he wrote to Roebuck, urging him to consider making Boulton a partner.

Roebuck was somewhat cool to the idea. He proposed to give Boulton the right to manufacture engines—but only in three counties.

Early in 1769, Watt's patent was granted. A month later, Boulton wrote to Watt: "I am obliged to you and [Roebuck] for thinking of me as a partner in any degree but the plan proposed to me is so very different from that which I had conceived at the time I talked with you upon that subject that I cannot think it a proper one for me to meddle with. . . . It would not be worth my while to make for three Countys only, but I find it very well worth while to make for all the World."[1]

The negotiations dragged on. Six months later, Watt wrote to Roebuck, explaining all the advantages that Boulton would offer. With a nod toward his own personality flaws, he concluded, "Lastly, consider my uncertain health my Irresolute and Inactive disposition My Inability to Bargain and Struggle for my own with Mankind all of which disqualify me for any Great Undertaking."[2]

Roebuck offered Boulton half of his own two-thirds interest, or a one-third share. It still wasn't enough. Watt became discouraged again. He spent less and less time working on the steam engine, and more and more time doing surveying work. His agile brain was diverted into another area: devising improvements to surveying instruments. There was a kind of satisfaction and certainty in the work, as he explained to Small: "The canal I had projected last winter for which an Act had been obtained was wanted to be begun under my inspection—I had now a choice whether to go with the experiments on the engine, the event of which was uncertain, or to embrace an honorable and perhaps profitable employment attended with less risk of want of success."[3]

As biographer H. W. Dickinson comments, "[Watt] never would take chances, he always played for safety, and was quite lacking in enterprise. It looks really as if he had less faith in his engine than had his friends. . . . Watt was so closely occupied with his survey work, which increased rapidly, that he could not find any time to devote to the engine, and consequently it came to a dead stop."[4]

Events outside of Watt's control were about to breathe life back into the project. Roebuck had to declare bankruptcy in 1773. Watt was able to get complete ownership of the Kinneil engine. Another part of the settlement involved Boulton, who was one of Roebuck's creditors. Boulton agreed to take Roebuck's share of the patent rather than money. The other creditors had no problem with that arrangement. None of them placed any value on Watt's engine.

In September that year, Watt received word that his wife was seriously ill. He rushed home, but she had died even before he had been notified. He was now a widower, with two young children. With little to keep him in Scotland, he moved to Birmingham the following spring. He took the Kinneil engine with him. Boulton found a place for Watt and his children to live. With Boulton's support, Watt plunged into full-time work with the steam engine and made rapid progress.

There was another obstacle. Watt's patent was already more than five years old. It would expire in eight more years. In Boulton's estimate, that didn't provide enough time to recover the necessary expenses before the patent would expire. He and Watt went to London to persuade Parliament to extend it. While there was a great deal of opposition, they received a 25-year extension—it even covered Scotland—on May 22, 1775. For Watt, the satisfaction was tempered with sadness. His great friend William Small, who had provided him with so much encouragement, had died not long before.

Boulton's infectious energy overcame Watt's natural hesitation. He pressed ahead with the development of two engines. By early 1776, the new partners had produced the first one. Located in a coal mine at Bloomfield, it passed its first test with flying colors. Working at 15 strokes a minute, it emptied 60 feet of water from the pit in under an hour.

Later that year, Watt made a brief return to Glasgow. He had a simple purpose: to find a wife. Almost nothing is known of Watt's relationship with Anne MacGregor—in all likelihood, he had already been acquainted with her. They were soon married, and the newlyweds returned to Birmingham.

Watt seemed to be on the right track. In Boulton, he had the right partner. His first successful engine appeared to demonstrate that he had the right idea. And even though he didn't particularly love his new wife, he believed that she was the right woman for him. He later wrote that marrying Anne was one of the best decisions he ever made.

Soon, however, many of his doubts would return.

Newcomen

Thomas Newcomen was born in 1663 in Dartmouth, England. After serving his apprenticeship, he opened his own blacksmith shop in Dartmouth about 1685. No one knows when he became interested in steam engines. According to one contemporary source, this interest developed without knowledge of Thomas Savery's Miner's Friend. It is likely that it came about when he visited the nearby tin and copper mines in Cornwall to sell and repair tools that the miners used. That would have given him firsthand exposure to the severe flooding problems that continually plagued them. Pumping by hand or by using horses was slow and laborious.

In 1705 Newcomen built a steam engine with the assistance of John Calley. A much improved version began operating at a coal mine in 1712. By then Savery had held his patent for several years. Even though Newcomen's engine operated under different principles and was much more effective than Savery's, Newcomen was considered to be infringing on the other man's patent. It didn't expire until 1733. The only solution was to form a sort of partnership. Savery would receive a royalty payment for every engine that Newcomen sold. Newcomen must have been upset by this arrangement, but it was the only way in which he could continue to sell his engines. Adding insult to injury, his engines were often called Savery engines because they were built under Savery's patent.

Not even Savery's death in 1715 helped. A group of investors quickly purchased the patent rights from his heirs. As a result, Newcomen never enjoyed more than a modest income from his invention. He had to continue making royalty payments.

Newcomen died in 1729. His name lives on in the Newcomen Society, an organization founded in London in 1920 to study the history of engineering and technology. An American branch was founded three years later. It is now completely separate from the English group.

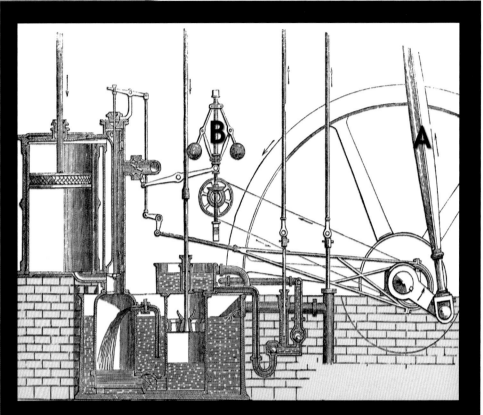

A drawing showing part of one of Watt's later steam engines. The crankshaft (A) provided power to run machinery. The centrifugal governor (B) was Watt's final improvement. With the governor, the engine could regulate itself. No one had to watch it.

4

The Rotative Engine

In 1777, the firm of Boulton & Watt set its sights on Cornwall, a region in the extreme southwest corner of England. The area was dotted with tin and copper mines, some of which extended a thousand feet or even deeper. More than 60 Newcomen engines were located there, but the mines often had to shut down during the rainy season. Even worse, there was little coal in Cornwall. The fuel had to be imported from other areas. That made it much more expensive to operate the machines.

The mine owners showed a great deal of interest in Watt's new engine. As a result, Watt spent most of the next four years in Cornwall. Each engine had to be erected and then fine-tuned so that it would work effectively. Watt worked out a unique method of payment. The great advantage of his engines was the saving in fuel costs. In many cases, Boulton & Watt engines were replacing Newcomen engines, so it was relatively easy to compute those savings. He decided that the mine owners would pay the firm one-third of those savings for 25 years.

Watt hated being in Cornwall. He disliked the people with whom he worked. Many were rough men who tried to underpay the firm or avoid payments altogether. Watt tried to avoid confronting them. He missed the stimulation of his friends in the Lunar Society, a group of the brightest minds in Birmingham who met regularly to discuss topics of interest (mostly scientific).

By 1780, conditions had improved. Boulton secured a much better house for the Watts. More importantly, he found a good assistant for Watt to help him in his dealings with the locals. The assistant, William Murdock, had impressed Boulton by appearing for his interview wearing a unique hat. It was made of wood. Murdock had fashioned it on a lathe he had constructed himself.

Murdock made an equally good impression on Watt. One reason was that he was a physically imposing man. When the Cornwall miners tried to intimidate him, he offered to fight them. None took him up on the offer.

The firm began turning a modest profit as they installed more and more engines. At least Watt, with his single-minded devotion to steam engines, thought so. Boulton had many enterprises going on and needed more money. Labor problems and other factors—including a fire at Soho that destroyed valuable equipment and damaged the plant itself—forced him to borrow heavily. At one point, he even risked the firm's most precious asset: the 1769 patent. That was one of the few times that the relationship between the two partners was strained.

Characteristically, Watt was in despair, envisioning the ruin of the company. "I thought I was resigning in one hour the fruits of my labour of my whole life—and that if any accident befell you or me I should have left my family destitute of the means of subsistence by throwing away the only jewel fortune has presented me with."[1]

Just as characteristically, Boulton saw an opportunity. "The people in London, Manchester and Birmingham are steam mill mad,"[2] he wrote back.

Always the visionary, Boulton had realized—much earlier than his partner—that the market for engines designed solely for pumping water was very limited. The potential for "rotative motion"—engines that could transform the up-and-down movement of the beam into circular motion, which in turn could drive other machines—was far larger. Watt had briefly referred to rotative motion in the application for his condenser patent. Boulton began encouraging Watt to develop this idea. He urged him to postpone his work on pumping engines even though it might lead to some short-term losses.

Watt may have grumbled at the goad, but his partner was insistent.

So in 1781—now back in Birmingham—Watt began a period of creativity virtually unprecedented in the annals of invention. First he developed the sun-and-planet motion. The "sun" and "planet" were two toothed interlocking gear wheels of the same size. The sun was attached to a much larger wheel. The planet was attached to the wooden beam. As the beam made its familiar up-and-down motion, it drove the planet around the sun. Every time the planet made one complete orbit around the sun, the sun itself rotated twice. So did the large wheel to which it was attached. With a belt attached to the large wheel, manufacturers now had the driving force they needed to run their machines. The belt provided power to a pulley system suspended from the ceiling, which in turn distributed power to other machines in the building.

Sun-and-planet gear wheels. The planet was attached to the beam, which the steam engine drove. The up-and-down movement of the beam caused the planet gear to move around the sun, which was fastened to a large wheel. The wheel in turn was connected to a belt that provided power for machinery.

This innovation was important because it freed factories from their dependence on a source of running water. In particular, it let England's growing number of textile manufacturers build wherever they wanted. Factories could now be located anywhere. They could be built in large towns and cities, where there was already a large population of potential workers. The factories created jobs, which in turn attracted even more people to the cities.

After the sun-and-planet, Watt turned his attention to another issue. The traditional steam engine was single-acting. Its downward motion gave the power stroke. The upward motion that followed was dead space in which the piston reset itself. Watt wanted to develop a double-acting engine, in which there was a power stroke on both the up and the down motions of the piston. That would generate more power and make the engine even more efficient. The principle was simple. Steam had to be piped into the cylinder above the piston to help push it downward, then introduced at the bottom of the stroke to push it up again. Watt—by this time showing few signs of the mental paralysis that had often gripped him during the early period of development—quickly devised a solution with a complicated series of additional pipes and valves.

The successful double-acting engine created a problem. In a single-acting engine, a chain connected to the piston pulled the beam down. But a chain could not push the beam back up. In 1784, he developed what he called parallel motion. Using his geometry skills, he devised a series of several flexible rods and levers. Now the piston could both pull the beam down and push it back up.

Watt was particularly pleased with this evidence of his ability. He termed it "one of the most ingenious simple pieces of mechanism I have contrived." He added that he was "more proud of the parallel motion than of any other mechanical invention I have ever made."[3]

A number of textile mills placed orders. The firm not only began to show a profit, it also avoided the financial crisis that Watt had feared. The always restless Boulton—who had recently soared aloft in a hot-air balloon, a craze that was attracting thousands of earthbound spectators—now thought about installing the engines where they would do the most good for people. He wanted to put them in factories that

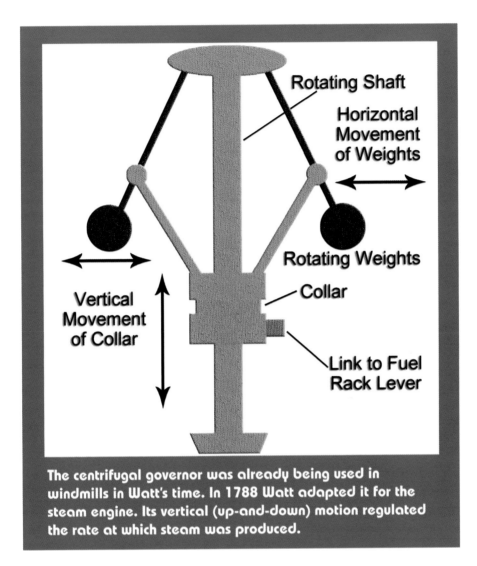

Rotating Shaft

Horizontal Movement of Weights

Rotating Weights

Collar

Vertical Movement of Collar

Link to Fuel Rack Lever

The centrifugal governor was already being used in windmills in Watt's time. In 1788 Watt adapted it for the steam engine. Its vertical (up-and-down) motion regulated the rate at which steam was produced.

produced the two primary dietary staples of that era—bread and beer—in England's main population center, the city of London. The partners installed engines in two London breweries. Boulton made sure that they received a great deal of publicity. King George III visited one and was impressed. The real showpiece was a corn mill that featured two of their largest engines. The building was equally remarkable. It was the first large structure to be made entirely of iron. The mill became highly successful. People traveled from all over Europe to see it.

It seemed that Watt's inventive genius had finally run its course. Late in 1785, he said, "I find it now full time to cease attempting to invent new things, or to attempt anything which is attended with any risk of not succeeding. . . . Let us go on executing the things we understand and leave the rest to younger men, who have neither money nor character to lose."[4]

But he wasn't quite ready to heed his own advice. In his mind, the engine still had a flaw. It required constant human supervision to keep it running efficiently. He adapted a device already in use in other applications, the centrifugal governor. It consisted of two small balls that spun around a central pivot. If the engine began to run too rapidly, the balls would spin faster. Centrifugal force would drive them away and upward from the pivot. That in turn would activate a steam valve, which would slow down the engine.

Watt also had to figure out a new pricing method. The old way, of calculating the fuel savings of Boulton & Watt pumping engines that replaced Newcomen models, didn't apply. The firm's new rotative engines weren't replacing older engines. In addition to waterwheels, they were often replacing horses that had been used as the "force" to power machinery in mills. Charging a premium based on the number of horses that would have done the same work seemed reasonable.

The concept wasn't new. Thomas Savery had figured that his Miner's Friend would replace two horses at any one time, or as many as a dozen on the basis of continuous operation. Watt wanted to be more scientific. A typical mill horse walked in a circle about 24 feet in diameter, exerting a pull of 180 pounds. Making two and a half circles in a minute, the horse generated 32,400 foot-pounds of force during that period, which Watt rounded up to 33,000. That became "one horse power." The firm soon calculated the power of its engines in terms of the number of horses that they replaced in theory. The more powerful the engine, the more horsepower it had—and the more they could charge.

Joseph Priestley

Matthew Boulton enjoyed hosting lengthy, leisurely dinners for friends such as Erasmus Darwin and William Small. He also enjoyed their stimulating conversations about a variety of scientific subjects—and the way that new advances in science could be applied to industry.

These dinners began attracting Birmingham's other important thinkers and manufacturers—including Watt soon after his arrival in 1774. While there were no formal rules for admission, all the members had wide-ranging interests and had to be willing to discuss these interests freely and openly. One reason for the success of their meetings was that the group never appears to have had more than 14 members. That way everyone had ample opportunity to speak up. Another reason was that they never discussed politics or religion. These were controversial subjects that could have provoked sharp differences of opinion.

They met once a month, rotating the site among the homes of the different members. These meetings lasted for up to six hours and were scheduled to coincide with the full moon. The moonlight enabled the members to find their way home in safety. The conjunction with the moon suggested their name—The Lunar Society— and the members jokingly referred to themselves as Lunatics. Today, we might call their meetings a form of networking. They freely gave each other useful advice in conducting their respective businesses.

Some of the members were

• Josiah Wedgwood, who developed an advanced manufacturing process for the elegant china dinnerware that still bears his name;
• Joseph Priestley, who is credited with the discovery of oxygen;
• William Withering, who discovered the beneficial effect that the plant digitalis has on heart conditions;
• John Baskerville, a printer who designed a typeface bearing his name that is still in common use today;
• John Whitehurst, whose interests ranged from geology to inventing an improved version of the toilet.

The Lunar Society met regularly until Boulton's death in 1809. At that point, the society lost much of its momentum. Four years later, it disbanded.

An engraving of James Watt. Its date is unknown. It probably was made relatively late in his life. By then he was very successful.

5

Lawsuits and Leisure

By 1790, the firm was doing well enough that Watt could think about buying a more luxurious home. He purchased a large tract of land in Birmingham and erected a mansion, which he named Heathfield. Eventually the estate encompassed 40 acres and included a garden, stables, and lodges. Along with Boulton, Watt was beginning to pull back from complete involvement in the business. In 1794 the firm of Boulton, Watt & Sons was formed; Watt's two sons, James and Gregory, and Boulton's son, Matthew, were now part of the company.

Watt also spent a great deal of time with lawyers. The English landscape was dotted with pirated copies of their steam engine. Often the threat of a lawsuit was enough to win—the owners would grudgingly pay the royalties. Other times they had to go to court. When that happened, Watt would be called on to provide testimony. Although the firm almost always won, these courtroom appearances were stressful.

When he was a boy, Watt had found peace from his problems by going into a corner of his father's workshop. Several decades later, he made a part of his Heathfield home into a workshop. There he could find the same peace by tinkering and performing scientific experiments for his enjoyment. The workshop became his retreat from the pressures of lawsuits, and even from his wife's compulsive tidiness.

In 1800, the patent for the separate condenser expired. By then, the firm had produced nearly five hundred steam engines. Both Boulton and Watt had become very wealthy. Though the ever-energetic Boulton remained active in several fields of endeavor even at the age of 72, Watt was content to retire.

Watt's last years were fruitful and enjoyable. In general his health was probably better than it had been for much of his life—perhaps because he no longer had to worry about money. He bought a large country estate in Wales. Freed from the compulsion to work all the time, he read a great deal and traveled frequently.

Watt was among the most honored men in England. He received an honorary degree from Glasgow University, was a member of the prestigious Royal Society of London, and became an associate of the French Academy. During one of Watt's trips to Scotland, he met the famous novelist Sir Walter Scott, who was known as the Great Magician. Scott was very impressed. He wrote, ". . . this magician [Watt], whose cloudy machinery has produced a change in the world the effects of which, extraordinary as they are, are perhaps only now beginning to be felt."[1]

Following a brief illness, James Watt died on August 19, 1819, at the age of 83. He was buried beside Boulton. Within a few years his admirers, believing that his contributions to the nation demanded public recognition, organized a fund-raising drive for a large statue. It was placed in Westminster Abbey.

By then another part of his legacy had become obvious. Some people began seeing the steam-driven factories as evil. The factories belched black smoke into the air. Working conditions there were sometimes dangerous and inhumane. While factory work is generally much safer today, there is still tension between the efficiency that machines provide and the monotony that operating them involves.

Still another of his legacies is connected with the watt, one of the primary measures of electrical energy, which is named after him. A 100-watt lightbulb, for example, casts much more light than a 50-watt bulb.

Born in Scotland in 1771, Sir Walter Scott became one of the most famous novelists of the 19th century. He is especially noted for writing the first historical novels, including *Ivanhoe* and *Rob Roy*. He died in 1832.

There can be no doubt about his importance to the Industrial Revolution. During Watt's lifetime, England's economy changed completely. It became based on large factories, rather than on craftsmen operating out of their homes or small companies located next to streams. This change wouldn't have been possible without Watt's major improvements to Newcomen's steam engine.

The sickly little boy who was bullied by his schoolmates, the man who often fell into the depths of depression, overcame his limitations to make a permanent impact on the world.

USS *Monitor*

It didn't take long for shipbuilders to realize the possibilities that steam offered. In 1801, a Scot named William Symington fitted a steam engine to a small boat and cruised the waters near Glasgow. Among the onlookers was an American named Robert Fulton. Fulton bought a Boulton & Watt engine and took it with him to the United States. In 1806, he began building a steamboat called the Clermont. Jeering passersby called it "Fulton's Folly." The following year, the boat made a successful trip up the East River in New York. Soon it began carrying paying passengers.

In 1819, the American ship Savannah became the first steam-equipped vessel to cross the Atlantic, though most of the trip was made using the ship's sails. By the middle of the century, dependable steam-powered passenger service had begun. These iron ships made the trip in half the time of sailing ships. One of the main technical advances followed soon afterward. Side-mounted paddle wheels were replaced by one or more propellers mounted underwater at the vessel's stern. By the end of the 19th century, scores of steam-powered passenger ships brought tens of thousands of immigrants from Europe to the United States. Thousands of cargo ships with steam power crisscrossed the globe.

Navies all over the world saw the advantages of steam power. Battles at sea would no longer depend on the wind. The U.S. Navy commissioned a steam and sail warship, the USS Fulton, in 1815. By the start of the Civil War in 1861, the Navy had a number of ships that utilized both sails and steam engines. One was the USS Merrimac. Confederate forces captured it soon after the war broke out. They began converting it into an "ironclad," a vessel covered with heavy iron armor and completely dependent on steam power, and renamed it the CSS Virginia. The plan became known to Union spies. Feverishly the Navy began constructing an ironclad of its own, the USS Monitor. The two vessels met at Hampton Roads, Virginia, on March 9, 1862, in history's first battle between armored warships. The outcome was a draw.

Chronology

1736	Born on January 19 in Greenock, Scotland
1753	Mother dies
1754	Moves to Glasgow, Scotland
1755	Moves to London to learn instrument making
1756	Returns to Glasgow
1757	Named Mathematical Instrument Maker to the University of Glasgow
1759	Opens shop in partnership with John Craig
1763	Opens new and larger shop
1764	Marries Margaret "Peggy" Miller
1765	Invents condenser
1766	Becomes a land surveyor; daughter Margaret is born this year or next
1769	Patents condenser; birth of son James
1773	Wife Peggy dies
1774	Moves to Birmingham, England
1775	Extends condenser patent; forms partnership with Matthew Boulton
1776	First engine, installed in Bloomfield, England, is a success; marries Anne MacGregor
1777	Begins selling engines in Cornwall; birth of son Gregory
1781	Develops sun-and-planet motion
1782	Patents double-acting steam engine
1784	Develops parallel motion
1785	Elected to Royal Society
1800	Condenser patent expires; ends active participation in business
1814	Elected as Foreign Associate of the French Academy
1819	Dies on August 19

Timeline in History

1662	King Charles II grants a charter to the Royal Society, England's first formal organization for the advancement of scientific knowledge.
1698	Thomas Savery patents the Miner's Friend, a steam pump used for drawing water out of mines.
1709	Abraham Darby begins using coke to smelt iron.
1712	Thomas Newcomen builds his first successful steam pump.
1728	Matthew Boulton is born.
1733	John Kay patents the flying shuttle, which speeds up the process of weaving cloth.
1735	English instrument-maker John Harrison invents the first practical marine chronometer, which helps sailors determine their location at sea.
1756	Britain and France begin Seven Years' War, which increases the need for crews on Royal Navy ships.
1760	George III becomes English king; he rules until 1820, the second-longest reign in English history.
1762	Matthew Boulton opens the Soho engineering works in Birmingham.
1764	James Hargreaves invents the spinning jenny.
1770	Richard Arkwright patents the water-powered spinning frame for producing cotton thread.
1779	Samuel Crompton invents the spinning mule.
1785	Edmund Cartwright patents power loom to weave cotton.
1787	The U.S. Constitution is adopted.
1789	George Washington becomes first U.S. President.
1807	Robert Fulton's steamboat *Clermont* begins regular passenger service.
1809	Matthew Boulton dies.
1829	English inventor George Stephenson introduces his steam-powered locomotive "Rocket," which pulls passenger carriages at speeds of up to 30 miles per hour.
1837	The steamship *Great Western*, designed by Isambard Kingdom Brunel, becomes the first vessel to cross the Atlantic using primarily its own power.
1855	Henry Bessemer's process for mass-producing steel is patented.
1862	Battle between USS *Monitor* and CSS *Virginia* (*Merrimac*) during the Civil War is the world's first naval combat between armored, steam-powered warships.
1866	I. K. Brunel's steamship *Great Eastern* lays the first transatlantic telegraph cable.
1869	Union Pacific and Central Pacific Railroads meet at Promontory Point, Utah, to complete the first transcontinental railroad line. The trains are powered by steam.

44

Chapter Notes

Chapter One   A Momentous Change

    1. Jenny Uglow, *The Lunar Men: Five Friends Whose Curiosity Changed the World* (New York: Farrar, Straus and Giroux, 2002), p. 497.

Chapter Two   A Perplexing Problem

    1. Jenny Uglow, *The Lunar Men: Five Friends Whose Curiosity Changed the World* (New York: Farrar, Straus and Giroux, 2002), p. 96.

    2. Ibid., p. 97.

    3. H. W. Dickinson, *James Watt: Craftsman and Engineer* (Cambridge, England: Cambridge University Press, 1935), p. 36.

Chapter Three   Trials and Tribulations

    1. Jenny Uglow, *The Lunar Men: Five Friends Whose Curiosity Changed the World* (New York: Farrar, Straus and Giroux, 2002), pp. 103–104.

    2. Eric Robinson and A. E. Musson, *James Watt and the Steam Revolution* (New York: Augustus M. Kelley, 1969), p. 62.

    3. Ibid., p. 64.

    4. H. W. Dickinson, *James Watt: Craftsman and Engineer* (Cambridge, England: Cambridge University Press, 1935), p. 71.

Chapter Four   The Rotative Engine

    1. J. G. Crowther, *Scientists of the Industrial Revolution* (London: The Cresset Press, 1962), p. 160.

    2. Ibid., p. 161.

    3. Ben Marsden, *Watt's Perfect Engine* (New York: Columbia University Press, 2002), p. 119.

    4. Ibid., p. 125.

Chapter Five   Lawsuits and Leisure

    1. Jenny Uglow, *The Lunar Men: Five Friends Whose Curiosity Changed the World* (New York: Farrar, Straus and Giroux, 2002), pp. 496–497.

Further Reading

For Young Adults

Bland, Celia. *The Mechanical Age: The Industrial Revolution in England.* New York: Facts on File, 1995.

Champion, Neal. *James Watt.* Chicago: Heinemann Library, 2000.

Clare, John. *Industrial Revolution.* New York: Gulliver Books, 1994.

Sproule, Anna. *James Watt: Master of the Steam Engine.* San Diego: Blackbirch Press, 2001.

Wilkinson, Philip, and Michael Pollard. *Ideas That Changed the World: The Industrial Revolution.* Philadelphia: Chelsea House, 1991.

Works Consulted

Crowther, J. G. *Scientists of the Industrial Revolution.* London: The Cresset Press, 1962.

Dickinson, J. W. *James Watt: Craftsman and Engineer.* Cambridge, England: Cambridge University Press, 1935.

Lord, John. *Capital and Steam-Power.* New York: A. M. Kelley, 1965.

Marsden, Ben. *Watt's Perfect Engine.* New York: Columbia University Press, 2002.

Robinson, Eric, and A. E. Musson. *James Watt and the Steam Revolution.* New York: Augustus M. Kelley, 1969.

Rolt, L.T.C. *Great Engineers.* New York: St. Martin's Press, 1963.

Turner, Roland, and Steven L. Goulden (editors). *Great Engineers and Pioneers in Technology. Volume 1: From Antiquity Through the Industrial Revolution.* New York: St. Martin's Press, 1981.

Uglow, Jenny. *The Lunar Men: Five Friends Whose Curiosity Changed the World.* New York: Farrar, Straus and Giroux, 2002.

On the Internet

James Watt and the Invention of the Modern Steam Engine
http://inventors.about.com/library/inventors/blwatt.htm

James Watt 1736–1819
http://www.geocities.com/Athens/Acropolis/6914/watte.htm

Lira, Carl. "Biography of James Watt."
http://www.egr.msu.edu/~lira/supp/steam/wattbio.html

———. "Brief History of the Steam Engine"
http://www.egr.msu.edu/~lira/supp/steam/

———. "The Double-acting Piston and the Rotative Engine"
http://www.egr.msu.edu/~lira/supp/steam/double.htm

The Impress Service
http://www.nelsonsnavy.co.uk/broadside7.html

The Lunar Society
http://www.lunarsociety.org.uk/

The Newcomen Steam Engine
http://www.technology.niagarac.on.ca/people/mcsele/newcomen.htm

Robin Hood—Bold Outlaw of Barnsdale and Sherwood
http://www.boldoutlaw.com

Thomas Savery
http://library.thinkquest.org/C006011/english/jsites/steam_thomas_savery.php3?v=2

Glossary

apprentice (uh-PREN-tiss)—a person who works with an experienced craftsman for a certain period of time in order to learn that craft.

capitalize (KAH-peh-tuh-lize)—to profit; to turn something to one's advantage.

carbon dioxide (KAR-bun die-OK-side)—a heavy colorless gas that comprises a tiny part of the earth's atmosphere.

centrifugal force (sen-TRIH-fuh-gul FORCE)—the tendency of an object moving in a circle to move outward from the center of the circle.

cistern (SIS-turn)—a container for water or other liquids.

digitalis (dih-jih-TAH-luss)—dried and powdered foxglove leaves; it stimulates the heart to beat more strongly.

entrepreneurs (on-truh-pruh-NYORS)—people who take on the risks and rewards of a business or other enterprise.

forge (FORJ)—a furnace used to heat metal so that it can be worked.

geometry (jee-AH-muh-tree)—the branch of mathematics that deals with lines, points, angles, and their respective measurements.

lathe (LAYTH)—a machine that continually turns, spinning a material (usually wood) so that it can be shaped using tools.

lucrative (LOO-kruh-tiv)—profitable, generating wealth.

provincial (pruh-VIN-shull)—limited in outlook; unsophisticated.

vacuum (VAH-kyoom)—space made as empty of air as possible to create low pressure.

versatile (VER-sih-tul)—able to understand a range of subjects or skills.

Index